E=mc²
The Hidden Formula for Success

Crystal City Publishing, LLC

Nevada/California
USA

$E = mc^2$

THE HIDDEN FORMULA FOR SUCCESS
THE MASTER KEYS TO GAINING A
DYNAMIC LIFE

BY

ARYEH YAHSHUA

Crystal City Publishing

P.O. Box 64-1181, Los Angeles, CA 90064

For information address: Crystal City Publishing, LLC. P.O. Box 64-1181, Los Angeles, CA 90064

Aryeh Yahshua
E=mc² The Hidden Formula for Success
First Edition: August 2013
Printed in the United States of America
ISBN: 978-0-9892485-0-1 (paperback)
ISBN: 978-0-9892485-1-8 (eBook)

Publisher – Crystal City Publishing, LLC.
www.crystalcitypublishing.com

Cover Design – Madison McClintock
www.madisonjmcclintock.com

Editing - Morissa Schwartz and Crystal City Editing Team

There are statements made
to land in the hearts
of the ones they're designed for.
(Super Mind 2012)

YAHWEH BEN YAHWEH BEN YAHWEH

ACKNOWLEDGMENT

YAHWEH thank you. There is nothing calculable in this physical or spiritual realm that comes close to how much you do and have done for me. It is incredible. Every day I thank you for your faith in me and in us.

To Crystal City thank you for your patience, understanding, help, counsel and encouragement.

To my best friend, teacher, supporter All-star, and mother, your contributions were invaluable. I love you. This wouldn't have manifested without you - Period.

To my dad Ray thank you for the tough love and laughs.

To my dad thank you for your wisdom and faith. Danielle for everything you do.

To my amazing friends and family, you know who you are.

CFY, I LOVE ALL OF YOU FOREVER.

To my brothers and sisters, you are all awesome don't ever stop dreaming and getting better. You can do ANYTHING. You cannot be limited anymore.

To Maddie thank you for being you.
I'd like to thank myself for listening to myself and the clues around me. Also thank you to all my Angels I come across on a daily basis. The people on this planet I learn so much from every day. Without your experiences added to the crossing of our lives, this couldn't have happened.
Also thank you for reading this. Let's become better every day. If together we stand together we shall never fall.

Contents

"A successful man is he who receives a great deal from his fellowmen, usually incomparably more than corresponds to his service to them. The value of a man, however, should be seen in what he gives and not in what he is able to receive."
ALBERT EINSTEIN

"No one saves us but ourselves. No one can and no one may. We ourselves must walk the path."
BUDDHA

Preface

This book will bring the formula $E=mc^2$ to life for its reader. You will begin to gain practical understanding as to why $E=mc^2$ reigns high as the ingenious formula in physics.

The very concepts given within the book will leap off the page as the reader gains clarity on the mental and spiritual understanding of the formula.

It gives rise to the Law of Attraction and other Universal Laws by teaching the reader the missing keys to use and manifest these laws.

Spirit is the key to all powers of mind. Thought lives and anxiously anticipates our command, if only we know how to self-manage it.

The reader will finally understand why situations occur, develop keys to deal with them and become the champion over their own life.

We are all born with an insurmountable power of greatness. It is dormant within waiting for the spark that will light its immense limitless power. It is here where the giant will arise. It is here where the genie will manifest. It is here that you will finally meet YOUR SELF.

$E=mc^2$ will be the light, which lights that spark.

DEDICATION

All the good people on the earth.

The kingdom of heaven is like a treasure hidden in a field.

CHAPTER 1
$E=MC^2$

1

CHAPTER 1 - E=MC²

What Is This?

Stop right now and ask yourself, *what is the meaning of E=MC²?* I mean, if you're like me, you've probably seen the equation a bunch of different times with no real clear definition of it.

Usually, when we feel something doesn't apply to us, we just put it on the backburner. We normally prioritize things in our lives. We take the important things and apply them to the forefront of our minds. The things we don't really understand or the ones not important, we just put it on the backburner. That was E=MC² for me.

The mere presence of equations overwhelms most people. Then there are some who sit back and reflect on the genius of equations. But, few try to understand the deeper meaning of them. When someone figures out an equation, usually that's the end of it. They have already figured out the answer.

So, what else is left? Well, if you're like me, when you heard the equation $E=MC^2$, your brain instantly changed the channel. You didn't really see a need to solve it, and all we were ever told was that Einstein was a genius when he created it. Why? What is it about this equation that would allow it to become immortalized as one the most memorable and symbolic equations. Even if you don't know much about it, you've seen it and those letters and one number are forever etched in your memory.

If someone asks you to explain what you know about $E=MC^2$, you might move into things you've heard like speed, light, power, war, bombs, etc. If you're like some people, you might not have a clue about this equation. You might say, "Well, it has to do with math, physics, and Einstein, right?" Then, there are some that just don't know and don't care. They say, "What does it have to do with me?" "What does $E=MC^2$ have to do with me?" And, that's the right question to ask. Everyone should ask, "What does $E=MC^2$ have to do with me?"

Many things we learned in school, we just didn't understand. We may have known the answers for test time, but that's it. I was this type of person who said, "Just get through this test, and I won't ever have to do this again." "Make it through this final, and I'll never have to use this information again." By the way, this is an absolutely horrible way of thinking. It is called cramming. The reality is you actually don't ever really get rid of the information. Your subconscious puts it on the backburner as *information not needed at the present time.*

I always looked at it this way. I asked myself, "Am I going to ever have to use this in the future?" I considered myself a critical thinker, so I would ask myself, "What do linear equations have to do with me?" "How were points, graphs, lines and formulas going to help me in the future?" "Will they assist me on the road to success?" I deduced, divided, and decided it was not going to help me at all. So, there you go: the backburner.

You see, as humans we have a way of using only the information we feel is important on a day to day

4

basis. We take most of what we are given as fact. We rarely research or seek for a deeper meaning. Since we only place the things we feel are relevant to us in the forefront of our minds, we truly miss out on so many things simmering unattended on the backburner. A dinner normally consists of meat, vegetables and breads. If you really want to gourmet it up, you add soups, salads, and desserts. The idea behind this is, although we may focus only on cooking the meat, the other items still exist and are essential to making our dinner complete. We forget there's more to a thing than meets the eye. True beauty is on the inside. Taking the time to discover the many uses to simple things often resorts in unpaved roads to your own harmonious balance or your missing link.

Now, here is your three-minute physics lesson. Physics is from a Greek word that means "nature." By definition, Physics is a part of natural philosophy and a natural science that involves the study of matter and its motion through space and time, along with related concepts such as energy and force. More importantly, it is the general analysis of nature, conducted in order to understand how the universe behaves.

A few years ago this would have meant nothing to me. I would have asked my questions, decided it didn't have anything to do with me and kept it moving. So, why is it important now? Why after all this time has physics and this journeyed equation resurrected itself back into my and your life?

It all has to do with the sentence in the last definition of physics. It says that physics is analyzing nature in order to understand how the universe behaves. Let's go deeper and flex your mental muscles. Physics deals with nature. Yes, nature deals with flowers, trees, etc. However, another definition of nature talks about your character, your personality, identity, qualities, spirit, universe, and composition. Composition means what are you made of. What are the thoughts in your mind? A synonym for universe is domain. Domain is where you live or more importantly where your thoughts live.

So, in looking at physics it is both the study of the outside world and your inside world. Physics allows you the ability to analyze your mind, your thoughts, qualities, character, and personalities. You are able to see how your nature affects your behavior, and how this behavior creates your life situations.

So now back to E=MC². . . The known answer to "what is E=MC²" is energy equals mass, times the speed of light, squared. Normally it would end right there. Isn't that mostly what we were taught? Unless you were in physics class or took another class, which taught you the physical meanings of the equation. How it affects mass and motion or how it was used in the creation of an atom bomb. That's what we were taught that it was used for; at least that is what I personally was taught. I mean, people say right now that if every nuclear warhead was released, the world would almost end as we know it, almost immediately. That physical force comes from the equation E=MC², but hidden within this same formula is an even greater mental power.

Now let me say this, I feel like in this new age of time, we are starting to expand on everything we've learned in the past in order to become better. We're progressively moving forward every day. We are making new discoveries and taking a closer look at life. We understand that there is more to us than flesh, skin and bones. There is something within. There is something more to us than meets the eye. And since there is something more to us, then there has to be a deeper understanding of all the information we have learned and been given.

There have always been two sides to everything positive and negative, up and down, good choices and poor choices, internal and external - all an eternal balance.

So with that being said, why were we only taught one side of $E=MC^2$? I mean, a mutual power has to be established in order for you to gain the full understanding of anything. If you don't learn both sides you walk around with a one-sided perception of everything in life. Maybe that's why the earth is tilted to one side. No just kidding.

But seriously, understand if an atom bomb could generate a mega-explosion in the world just think what power you can have with the understanding of how to apply its mental forces to your own world – your life.

$E=MC^2$ is an equation. This means it equates to something. If it equates to something, this means it relates to something or connects you to something and even simplifies something for you. How many times have you said or heard, "life is hard." While this may be true in many aspects, there has to be balance to the hardships in life. There has to be a balance; that's the way that our world works. Positivity and negativity, an easy life must balance a hard life. It is the other side of the equation. The key is having the ability to unlock the door to the other side, and where does this door lead?

I didn't understand just how close we are all related to this equation. Each one of us, carefully woven in the silk-like thread of E=MC². My journey with this equation would truly shatter and rebuild everything I thought I knew about myself. Others who have learned its secrets feel the same. It is a master key to an ensemble of doors. Every opportunity will open itself to you. Just think this equation has been in our faces all this time? Like a gem covered in the dirt and shroud environment. There it sat truly a diamond in the rough. There hidden in plain sight within the pages of our books laid the underlying force of the Law of Attraction and all Universal Laws. It is the secret to success and the easy life.

Chapter 2
Are You Sleeping with the Enemy?

Chapter 2 - ARE YOU SLEEPING WITH THE ENEMY?

Are You Sleeping with the Enemy and How Did You Get Here?

This question immediately breaks down barriers in your life. Answering it **truthfully** will affect you in ways you cannot imagine. Even so, I am certain we have all been guilty of this.

Everyone's immediate reaction to the question "are you sleeping with the enemy" is always, "absolutely not; I am no cheater, never been a cheater, never going to be a cheater." Or if you are a cheater in your relationship, you may just sit in silence.

When I ask, "are you sleeping with the enemy?" This does not refer to asking about adultery or being disloyal to someone in a relationship. This refers to being unfaithful to your own self.

See, it's always the simplest things in our regular lives, which can affect us in the most extreme ways.

There are little things about us, which go unnoticed until we are forced to notice them. For example, we have all these bones and joints. We don't really think about or appreciate them, until something's wrong with one of them. Often we just say our foot with no regard to the intricate details which are a part of the foot. You don't really understand how much your big toe means, until you injure it in some kind of way. You then realize the big toe is essential for walking and standing. I guarantee you, no one values their metatarsals, unless they have a lisfranc injury and see one of their feet fold in half. This was my first awakening on noticing small things. A small injury can completely change in your life. The small things must work for the big things to work efficiently. In most cases, the answers to all big things are right in the small things we do or don't do every day.

Let's examine this in daily action. While sitting down for lunch one day, I ran into a good friend who, in my eyes, is a supremely fantastic artist. Our conversation eventually went to his talents and what he was doing with them. We talked about what he had done and what he had in the works. He told me he had done a couple things, had some fantastic ideas to do more, but he didn't have the time to do any. So, he ultimately generated nothing. We conversed a little more, said our good-byes and went on about our business.

Later on that evening, I took a trip to see one of my favorite couples. It always gave me great energy to see them together. They complemented each other so well. So much so, that you could just feel their love just by watching them interact. However, that day when I saw them, things were different. As they came through the door, the change was very apparent. We went about our normal greetings and began a conversation. When the wife stepped out to answer a call from work, this was my chance. I seized the opportunity to find out what was missing or what was going on.

As soon as she stepped out, I looked at my friend dead in the eyes and I said, "Alright, what's going on?" He laughed and replied, "Oh, everything's all good." "There is something a little different about you guys," I said. "The energy just feels really different." He laughed for a minute, and then looked away, looked back at me and said, "There's really nothing I can keep from you, is there?"

He told me, they wanted to have a child. They believed a child was what their relationship was missing. They talked and talked about it, but always got caught up in other things putting off having a child. At that moment, the wife returned and we changed the conversation. While we went on having a good time and conversation, I sat there thinking, "why this had become an issue for them?" I left them and walked towards my house. I had a lot on my mind.

As I made my way down the street, walking towards the bus stop, I heard a woman yelling about 2 or 3 yards in front of me. She was berating and yelling at her phone, talking to a friend, about how a man could leave a woman for being overweight. She was hysterical. She looked miserable, crying with makeup running. She was pretty torn up about the situation. Yet, this woman was holding a bag of fast food. I won't name the brand. I'm not trying to throw any companies under the bus. It seemed the guy had just outright told her, "She wasn't the person he met." "She had gained a lot of weight. He didn't like it and didn't want to deal with it anymore." The woman explained how she was trying to lose weight, while eating her fast food! She just could not understand why she was not losing weight.

I then looked to my right, and there was a guy explaining to his girlfriend how he was going to quit smoking. You could tell she had heard it before, but he kept trying to reassure her that this was the last time for sure. This was to be the end of his smoking he assured her with a pack of cigarettes in his hand. At that moment, I questioned my own happiness.

The bus came. I sat in the front of the bus wanting to get off as soon as possible. I needed to be alone. I needed to think about all I had seen and heard earlier in the day.

At home, after doing a little meditation and asking myself what to do, I told myself. This might sound crazy to some people, but I talk to myself and answer myself. So I said to myself, "Look around at everything we've seen and heard in the day, then figure out what was similar?" "What was the pattern in everything we saw in the day?"

There it was right in front of me. I realized it at that moment. Many of the things we need in life are right in front of us, but we are farsighted. We see things afar, but we don't see the ones right in in our immediate vision. For everyone I had encountered this day, the answers were right in their face. However, their vision was too impaired to see. Many of the answers that we are looking for in life can be answered by looking in the mirror. The answers begin by looking within.

Many people look outside for excuses. They want to blame someone or something else for challenges. They are looking outside themselves instead of looking within. This type of thinking leads one to believe that the answers are somewhere else.

Everyone I had encountered during the day reflected this type of thinking. They like me were "sleeping with the enemy."

We were all cheaters. Yes, that's right. I was a cheater, and so was almost everyone else. Everyone was cheating around me. People I didn't know, the people I knew, everyone. We were all twisted in the silent chaos of infidelity.

Understand this statement that I'm getting ready to give you. Understand it, know it, live it, and embrace it. The statement I am about to give you, post everywhere. Make sure you see it daily. Make sure everyone you know hears it. This statement itself will help you with many of the challenges that you come across in your life. Are you ready? Here it goes.

Procrastination kills Creation; it is the enemy of imagination.

Let's say that again: procrastination kills creation. It is the enemy of imagination. Say that over, and over, and over to yourself until it's fixed in your mind.

Procrastination is a villain - the number 1 serial dream-killer in this world. Imagination creates and creates, only to watch procrastination creep in the back door and just destroy a beautiful construction.

Let's look at the last examples: plain as the sky being blue. And here's another hint before we go onto this. There is a purpose for everything in your life. Every person, all you've done, every encounter has a reason. The answers will be hidden there. You need only to ask yourself the right questions. Now let's reflect.

In my first encounter with my long-time friend, who has great artistic talents, he was not applying them. He had put them on hold to get another job and create more money. Nothing is wrong with that. Nothing is wrong with getting another job to create more money, if it is needed. But you must prioritize. We sat there for 45 minutes to an hour talking about extracurricular activities. He had an abundance of time for extracurricular activities and fun. However, he saw absolutely no time to work on his talents and skills. Hmmm…There was no time in all that fun to maybe paint a picture, or do any of the things that he had once dreamed of doing. He was content with just complaining about it.

So, let's think about this. If his recreational time was just cut in half, or by a third, he could use that time to paint. After years of time being put aside to work on the things he really wanted to do, a little of that dream would soon be a reality. It's literally impossible for it not to be. If you set aside one-third of your fun time or extracurricular activities to work part-time on your talents, over time your dream will begin to manifest.

Next, the spectacular couple, who were feeling something, was missing in their relationship. They had great careers. They created a life together and now were considering a child. They even moved to a larger place to make room for the child. However, they forgot one key element: making the child.

This may sound silly, but it was true. They had taken all the steps for a future of having a child. Yet, they had done nothing towards it in the present day. They were content with their normal routines. No doctor's visits. No change in birth control. No preparation for present day. They just hadn't done it. Simply put, they didn't change their routine. They had a quiet resolve of discontent in the relationship, because they did not stop to look at themselves.

When they changed the routine and they did, it was an easy fix. They had a beautiful baby girl. Now, their relationship is harmonious again.

On to the next story, considering the woman on the phone was holding a fast food and complaining about the way her boyfriend felt about her weight. Now I'm not condoning in any way, shape, or form breaking up over weight problems. That's just ridiculous. What I am saying is, was she considering her actions? If she was serious about losing weight, was she doing the necessary things? Was she working out? If she didn't have time to go to a gym, was she eating healthy? She was not. Sometimes (most of the time) you have to be truthful with yourself. Ask yourself the tough questions. Like, are you continuously trying to find the easy way out?

On to the guy who was sitting on my right. He talked about no longer smoking. He said he would quit soon. He seemed almost annoyed that he had to even deal with it at that moment. Wouldn't the easy fix for him be to take the steps to stop smoking? Instead, he sat explaining how he would stop one day, while holding a new pack of cigarettes in his hand.

Again, it is imperative for us to be honest with ourselves. What routine can we change today, this morning, tonight, or in the morning? What can you change or create to better your life or situation? Really, really think about this.

You will find a lot of the excuses we give, are really just us saying, "It's just not important to us right now."

Let's put it this way. If your house is on fire, I guarantee your first initial reaction isn't to grab your refrigerator, and drag it through the door. You react to what's in front of you right then and there in emergency situations. If your house is on fire, you're going to get out as fast as possible. That's what's important right now. We easily and unconsciously respond correctly to the things that are important to us "right now."

So ask yourself, "What is important right now?" When you do, you will realize that you have been sleeping with the enemy probably since birth. You must prioritize what's important. Is it important for you to have extra income, or build a company, or lose weight, or be athlete, be a better mother or father? Then ask yourself, "What is stopping you from achieving your goals right now?" The truthful answer would be - you. It is just you and your old familiar friend: procrastination.

Look at yourself right now. Are you lying with procrastination, right now? Are you doing the important things needed to change your life? You see, procrastination knows a simple truth that you may or may not fully understand. **You Are a Live Wire!**

CHAPTER 3
Live Wire

CHAPTER 3 = LIVE WIRE

You are, whether you know it or not, a live wire.

Yes you. Everyone reading this book right now is a live wire. The conscious activity of you just reading this book is caused by the live wire within you.

You are constantly, day in and day out, turning and burning energy – whether you know it or not. Your body is lined with a circulatory system. The root word to circulatory is circuit. You are a circuit system. You are a walking, talking, breathing, dancing, and laughing circuit.

There are simple things which happen every day to prove this. You drag your feet on carpet, then shock someone with the energy from your body. Have you ever thought, "Wow, I just generated electricity and transferred it to another person in the form of an electrical shock. How did I do that?"

Another example is someone walks into a room angry. Your body picks up the waves vibrating from that person almost immediately. You look over; see his clinched fists, his fixed eyes and his stern upper lip. Your mind says, "Hey, stay away from that guy. That guy is pissed off." Literally, you pick up the transmitters he's giving off. You can pick up when a person is upset without them saying a word. You can feel it; you can feel energy coming from them.

In a balloon test, you rub a balloon on your hair; it will stick to you using magnetic friction. We each have electromagnetic currents running through us. There is an electronic system you have radiating through and around you.

Have you ever heard someone say, "Hey, that guy is magnetizing." Unconsciously, they are talking about the unseen magnetic force one shows in attracting to themselves the things or people they desire. Speaking of magnets since you are a live wire, you are constantly generating, pulling and pushing things to you or away from you.

For example, I eat lunch daily at one of my favorite restaurants. The food is amazing and everyone likes to go there. The service is good; however, because of the demand the food takes a little longer to get to you. April a female waitress, constantly complains about how she gets terrible tables all the time. The people yell at her. They are impatient and extremely demanding. I began to watch her as I went there for lunch daily. Day in and day out, she'd get these crazy off the wall tables. The most ridiculous things would happen to her involving these tables. Issues and problems seemed to be magnetized to her. It came to a point where she just fully expected it, and she got exactly what she expected.

Another waitress Kim, who works at the same restaurant, was having a different experience. Kim's section is right next to the April's. She too had difficult tables with people who yelled and got angry about the wait. However, she was completely unaffected by it. One day, I decided to sit in Kim's section instead of April's. I watched as she gracefully handled each table. I asked Kim jokingly, "what are you saying to those upset customers who are yelling at you? It always seems they are calm and happy once they leave your section." She simply replied, "I tell myself every day before I come in, no matter what, I'm going to have a great shift. I say, people love me, and I'm good at what I do."

She continued to say, "When I get an upset customer, I use my softest voice to let them know I am here to serve them. I ask what I can do to help them during the wait." I make them laugh. I share a story. I ask questions. I do whatever I can do to keep their minds off the wait time. I am happy and I desire to make them happy. She fully expected things to go well, and they do.

How many times have you felt like bad things were specifically happening to you? Everything seems to go wrong. It may start with bad hair in the morning and end with a flat tire in the evening. When it rains, it pours. Right? Wrong! You are attracting these things.

How many times have you thought to yourself, "Am I doing this?" Most people don't do this. It is easier to blame an outside source. They never look to see why their live wire is magnetizing a positive or negative energy?

Sometimes, we don't want to take responsibility or admit that many of the things happening to us are in our control. Whether you like it, believe it or act on it, you are still a live wire, with a central component called "your mind" attracting both positive and negative charges. Denial won't change this.

You see no matter what, your system is constantly picking up frequencies. The only way to counteract some of these frequencies is becoming conscious of them. You must know that all of this exists, so you can start to control it. Now that you have just heard these words, or read these words, you have become conscious of them. It has been told to you. Now, you can say, "Oh, well I don't believe that", and that's fine. But things are still going to happen to and for you. In a world that's motion, you can only progress or regress there is no standing still. The key is asking yourself, "who is in control?"

**Just like any power system you must be turned on.
You must be made conscious.**

An example of this is, what if you had a family
member leave you their house and a letter in a will?
The house is free and clear. You grab the deed, stuff
the letter in your jacket pocket and head to the
appraisers. You find out the house is worth about
one hundred fifty thousand dollars. This family
member was always known for hoarding and
collecting junk. You hadn't visited them since you
were a child, yet even then you always noticed they
had lots of stuff in the house. You would look at it all
for hours wondering how they had collected all of
this junk. The house was in good condition and could
be sold. However, as you expected, it was filled with
junk. After sorting and cleaning things up a bit, you
decide to give a lot of the things in the house away
and focus only on the sale of the house. You have a
yard sale giving most things away for only one dollar.
Anything not sold you give away and just trash the
things no one wants. Just to get it out. You end up
cleaning everything out and sale the house for one

31

hundred and fifty thousand dollars. You are happy. Here is a relative you barely knew helped you gain one hundred fifty thousand big ones.

A couple weeks later after the sale of the house, you hear antique collectors are in the city. A friend comes by your house and tells you they got two hundred and fifty thousand dollars for the ten items they bought from your yard sale. He also says the collectors say these are some of the greatest finds they've come across in a while. He urges you to take pieces you have to the show the collectors to find out their value. You have none.

At that moment, you recall the letter and open it. Your relative writes that you have always been their favorite grandnephew, although you didn't visit much. They recall how as a child, you loved to look at all of the art in the house. They also tell you how many people thought it was junk. However, it was priceless pieces they had collected over a number of years. They end the letter by saying they were leaving you a house valued at only one hundred fifty thousand or so. Inside the house there were pieces worth more than a million. You get a sickening feeling.

In this example, with you being the house, often we are only concerned with the value outside the body. We have no regard for the treasures within our bodies.

With everything you do, every thought, every word, every action you are intellectually instilling a power consciousness inside of yourself. Just think something in your life has magnetized you to this book. Because of this magnetism you have been mentally promoted, congratulations. Go ahead, take a minute to just relish in your own greatness; I'll give you a pause.

Again, congratulations! You have been promoted. You now know that you are a power system, a live wire. You see, wires help power this whole world from computers, to lights, you name it. The world runs on circuits – period. That's because we live in a circuit world.

Embracing Not Miss Using Power

Some people take power and they completely abuse it. The minute they think they hold the power. They automatically look down on others. You cannot do this. We all have this power. You must use power for good. If not, you will attract the negative repercussions of power. When you are in a position of power, it puts you also in a position of responsibility.

Although you are now a little more conscious, the more enlightened you become the more you realize all live wires need each other. We increase in power by sending out positive charges to one another. We all are power grids. The faster we can become conscious of each other's greatness, the faster we evolve as a species.

You should let other people know they are great. Let them know they can control, magnetize and attract anything they want. Bring it up in light in conversation. Share this information with others. Spread this knowledge to everyone. Remember, we all are power grids. We each have to turn our power on.

For those of you who now have your power on, you might be thinking, "What's next?" Power is not all the same. Like light bulbs, we all have different watts and volts. Everyone shines differently. It depends on your input. Input is crucial. The wrong ones can send you spiraling down the rabbit hole. The right ones can jumpstart your dreams.

CHAPTER 4
Field the Dream

CHAPTER 4 - FIELD THE DREAM

Understanding you must not sleep with the enemy and with your new live wired turned on power grid. You must now **field the dreams.**

Like I told you before, procrastination knows the secret. Procrastination knows that you are a power grid. The only thing it does is attaches itself to you. When you are sitting, doing nothing at all, or putting things off, you are attracting sitting, nothingness and idleness to yourself. Your mind becomes idle. Nothing comes from it. It is at a constant sitting or rest state.

In order for you not to find yourself sleeping with the enemy, you must do the opposite. You must field the dreams. You must take thoughts and implement them. You must create some kind of action; you must start.

The signs have always been all around us. We've heard plenty of sayings, such as "you reap what you sow, sow bad seeds, get bad harvest". Look at this if you sow lazy seeds, you get lazy harvest, or if you sow unproductive seeds, you get unproductivity. You can only get out what you put in. So, if all you do is sit on the sofa, you will get exactly what comes from sitting on the sofa – which is nothing. You might get a little comfort, but nothing towards building a great life, spiritual or mental growth, a business, getting the car you want, or moving into the house you saw.

You can't do anything without applying some kind of effort into getting what you desire. You must field your dreams. A field is an open plain or land ready for planting seeds, thoughts or ideas. The active work of a fielder is not only planting the crops. They are constantly de-weeding, watering and nourishing the crop, until they gain a great harvest.

You must take your thoughts and ideas then say to yourself, "this is what I desire or want." Next, you must start doing the necessary things to obtain those ideas. First you must act like you are already in possession of the thing you want. There must be action. You must take the ideas and take a step to gain them in faith.

The body, without spirit, is dead, so faith without works is also dead. This is a big comparison. Just think about this for a moment. If your body didn't have a spirit, you no longer exist. The same with having faith in something, but no action make it happen. It causes that thing to not exist. It will never come into existence with wishful thinking. You must plant a seed in the field, cover it with dirt, water it, de-weed it and nourish its growth. Very little or nothing comes from merely throwing a seed on the ground. You can have all of the belief in the world, but if you do not work towards it nothing will grow. Your idea is a dead. It is without life.

You are a body. There are things inside your body that must tick. They must work. Your heart must beat, your lungs must breathe air or else you die. When your spirit leaves your body – you're dead. It doesn't matter how good your body was working with no spirit inside, the thing that gives life, you are no more.

Looking at your idea as a body, you must put forth the works to generate life. The spirit works inside on your ideas and thoughts, and then brings them to life. Your works will generate life inside the body of your idea. Spirit is also courage and action. You must give your idea action. You must have the courage to act.

Now for me, this was a little difficult. I thought I had kind of a clear grasp on it; however, it had to be explained a little bit simpler. My mentor told me you must look at your idea as if you were getting ready to birth a baby. You may not know how that baby is going to turn out in the end. The only things you can do is love and give that baby the things it needs with the faith of knowing it will turn out beautiful.

A baby cannot eat a slice of pizza. If you try to feed a baby a slice of pizza the whole thing is not going to go well. You must feed the baby food to help it grow. You must do the little things before your baby can take on big things. Now some babies grow faster than others. Some babies grow taller than others. It all depends on you and what you're doing. You must do what you are able to do. You must take some action.

You must begin by setting goals. Set small goals. Often people sabotage themselves by setting unobtainable goals. Win small victories first, by setting attainable goals. When you reach these goals, confidence will grow quickly seeing your accomplishments.

Don't be reckless. Don't just jump up and quit a job or do something that will cause strain in your life. Recklessness and chaos only leads to more recklessness and chaos.

But do go ahead and start putting forth the work in fielding the idea. You must do it in a way to where your livelihood is not threatened. You might have a hard time planning for a successful idea, when your lights are getting turned off. We must be wise.

You want to keep a harmonious balance between your life and whatever idea that you have.

Remember you and your baby are in a new relationship. You must bond and nurture it. You must take care of the things that are needed. You can cut one bad habit to gain more time to work on what you want to do. Now, that's awesome thinking.

It's very difficult to work while stressed. I know for a fact that many, many of us are stressed. You must learn, inculcate and know "if you see it, and you believe it then you can achieve it, just roll up your sleevage." It sounds funny, but it's very true.

As people say, "you just gotta do the work". You have to plant the seeds. You have to start the diet. You have to do the outline. All of these things will help you in whatever you're trying to do. It starts with you and you must start.

You must remember **Procrastination Kills Creation and is the Enemy of Imagination**. If you don't start, you are sleeping with the enemy of your own imagination. Just like any person, if you cheat on your imagination, it will soon leave you. You will no longer get the great ideas, opportunities or even care about changing your life. You will become content with life as it is. You will become the person who says, "My life is okay. I don't need anything else." And you will be right, because whatever you think is what you get.

Now for the person who is willing to put in the effort to practice on the field of life daily nourishing the crops? They will reap excellent results.

Like the movie says, "if you build it, they will come." If you practice, if you water it, if you feed it, if you remove the weeds of negative thoughts, your field of thoughts and ideas will grow.

Now let's look at this for a minute. There is something very, very powerful in what I just said. It says, "If you build it, they will come." Did you catch that? It says "if **you build** it", not "when you." The "when you" is important yet. The mega-statement full of hidden gems is, if you take the action to build it. This is a pure game-changer when you truly understand it, and you will as we go along. But first, you must understand everything.

Chapter 5
Energy

Chapter 5 – ENERGY

Energy is everything...Everything is made of energy.

The question is, "What is Energy? This question cannot be answered in simplified terms. It is a combination of many realms and various planes. It deals with the physical or natural world, mental world, emotional world and spiritual world. It also shows up on all levels of intelligence. It makes up the natural and the supernatural. It is an awesome power, which regulates everything and encompasses this world.

With this all being said the next question should be, "perfect, what does that mean for me?" And my response is, "Energy's power is working in your life, every day, whether you are conscious of it or unconscious of it." Energy is so powerful. The right kind of energy can give you phenomenal power of mind, words and action. The wrong kind of energy can affect generations of people, and I do mean generations. You will understand why I say this later in the chapter.

It has been proven that humans emit energy. There's even a method to measure the energy in your body called a **Human Energy Conversion Formula**, which is H-E. It is the working of your metabolism and any exertion that comes out about a daily average of 12,500 KJ: a metabolic rate of 80 watts. Since we are not all science majors, this basically means each of us produce 80 watts of energy on a constant basis every day, while sitting idle. Can you think of anything else that produces energy of 80 watts? Oh, that's right, light bulbs. Light bulbs give light with the use of 80 watts of energy. You are an energy source and one of the most powerful energy sources. You use 80 watts of energy and you light up and go throughout your day.

Without your 80 watts of energy, you would cease to exist. You would be nothing – you literally turn into nothingness. I'm being very serious. During normal human activity, we are all using more than 80 watts a day in power. Now I love breaking movie codes, so here's another one right at you. For those who have seen, "The Matrix", this should shed some light on what some of us didn't know at the time when we saw that movie. What was the whole situation for the movie? What was the most upsetting thing or event of the whole movie?

If anyone has seen the Matrix, you may remember – it was the **humans** that were powering the Matrix. They were the power source. They were plugged in just like an electrical source. In fact, they had the outlets or plugs starting in the back of the head and going straight down their backs. The machines were using humans as energy. Without doing any activity just lying there in their pods, these humans were providing energy for the machines to operate and move on. Just shear mind energy. By only using their minds, these unaware humans lying in pods inside of the Matrix were putting off more than enough energy for the machines to use. This is symbolic of real life. This movie showed the truth. You are a live wire. For all of you doubters saying,

"I'm not a live wire" doubters, yes, it is true. Look it up for yourself. You'll find it under - **Human Energy Conversion Formula.**

We are a mere 20 watts under a bright light bulb. Our constant rate is 80 watts. Now let me light your mind again. Did you catch that little reference? For a difficult task or hard work, a person can generate thousands of watts for a few seconds. Yes, you heard me. A person can generate thousands of watts. Now, 746 watts is considered horsepower. So that means you, yes you, can giddy up past the power of horsepower many times.

This is amazing. You are amazing. It is even said that people for example: fit people, those exercising and even those in entire thought can generate around 1,000 watts, and can stay that way for minutes. There has never been any set period or output limit on the human power potential. We are only growing and getting better. As our minds become more and more conscious, as we become more and more alive, we start to generate more and more energy output. This is why you see most of the previous records once held are falling every other year. Records continue to get broken constantly, sprint records are being broken, high-jump records are being broken, and these records are constantly broken because we are becoming more and more powerful. We are becoming more and more alive, therefore being able to exert more energy and do more than those that came before us.

When asked why don't you see horses on the freeway? The obvious answer is because we have evolved. So, ideas for inventions evolve, but we don't? Horses at one point were a primary means of transportation. Now we have many means of transportation depending on where you need to go and the access you have. We've gotten better, we've advanced, we've moved on, and we always are going to continue to do so. Energy is motion. In a world of motion, you cannot be stagnant.

Now some may say watts are a measure of power, not energy. Alright, so that's when you politely grab a J.I. Rodale Synonym Finder, copyright in 1986. Go to page 352, find energy. You will find many synonyms such as: vigor, vitality, stamina, get up and go, intensity, force, and – *ah, there it is* – **power**, energy is all of these and more.

Now, I can go on and on about E as Energy, but we're just going to get to what matters in the equation for this book's purpose. Energy is everything. It can dance around and move around wherever it wants. It can also seem still by slowing down. Although, it doesn't really stop, it just slows down. Energy also has positive or negative charges and power. And both the positive and negative uses are balanced intense power.

Now, ask yourself, "How can I use energy for positive gain?" Remember, everything is motion and either you're putting energy into doing a whole lot or a whole lot of nothing, you're still using energy and a lot of power. You're either sleeping with the enemy, or you are not.

But know this for sure, we all have this energy. We all have this power. Do you hear that? We are all Ener-gy. We all have this Inner - G. This inner - G is your inner - God power. This is our Inner God self. For those of you who now have just jumped up out of your seat, and said "WHAT?" let's go right back to page 352 of that same Synonym Finder and look at Energy again. As you continue to look at the synonyms, you will see **spirit**. When you go to page 1145 in the same resource and look up spirit, you will see under spirit that it says, "God." Our inner - G is our inner spirit – our inner God power.

This is probably why in the Bible in the book of Corinthians 3:16 says, "Do you know that you are the temple of God, and that the Spirit of God dwells in you?" Then in the book Psalms 82:6 says, "I have said, you are Gods, and all of you are children of the Most High." It didn't say some – it said all. If you look up spirit, one of the synonyms of spirit is the breath of life. So as long as you breathe and have life, you possess the power of God. You have this power - this energy.

You see, there are many different terms for energy that people use. The law of attraction and many others learn laws and methods. But often these methods do not work for many people. This is because they were looking all over for answers, when all of the answers are within. They are looking to external solutions rather than looking within at themselves. They should look to their inner-G – their inner God power. It is here that real power resides. Like I said, awareness of power is what helps to create more power. If you do not know that you are power, you can't use it.

You are now aware of your inner God power. When you need something, you can look no further than in the mirror at yourself. Once you begin to look inside you will see and find the things that you need to see and find.

In fact, it is your absolute birth right to be able to look inside of yourself and pull out whatever miracle you need to have accomplished. It is all you. It is the choice that you make. The energy – inner G is going to be there and it's going to keep moving. Either it's going to lay dormant and continue to do the things it normally does unconsciously such as helping you to breathe, make you heartbeat, and assisting you with normal motions like walking. Or you are going to change your old thinking, grab hold of these new ideas of you as energy, the Inner - G, power, acknowledge the God Power and CHANGE YOUR LIFE to get the things that you want.

You can say right now, "I take control of this awesome power." "I inherit this, and from this point on, I'm going to create whatever it is that I set my mind to do."

When you really think about this, you begin to understand there is nothing you can't do. The possibilities are endless, and we are just getting the party started. What's next will truly blow your mind.

Chapter 6
Equals

Chapter 6 – EQUALS

Equals in the Formula E=mc²

Two friends very close to me decided, "You know what, enough talking, let's just do it together. Let's make the commitment, and we're going to lose weight together." They made an elaborate plan consisting of dieting, working out, being active, and more. Then they started the same day. Boom, they were off doing their thing, being conscious of their health, what they ate, exercise, and helping each other out.

About 11 to 12 weeks later, when I saw them again one was significantly smaller than the other. Through an exchange of information, I found out that one slipped back into old habits, and the other held strong. One had lost over 25 pounds more than the other. If we created a formula for this, it would be: person A worked out and ate right for two weeks out of the twelve weeks, and lost about 3 to 4 pounds. Person B changed their thinking, their habits and actions for over twelve weeks. With this new eight week change, they lost about 30 pounds.

I tell you this story to let you know this, there's equalization in everything. There is always an equal, a balance, in all things. There absolutely has to be a reaction universally for every action.

There is divine order: balance in all things. You see, many of us left school thinking the math we learned would be utilized to count money, on a job, and only as necessary. When the truth is the complete opposite, because math is all around us, equations are all around us, equalization and balance are all around us. The key is in knowing what you are looking for and at.

Let's look at it this way. There was one little pig, and this pig knew a wolf was coming. So this pig built a house out of straw. One pig plus straw, then one hungry wolf who was able to blow down the straw = what? The answer is one captured pig.

Now let's look closer into this, because there are things all around us that we may not see. Things are always more than what you see with your eyes, so we must see or comprehend with our minds.

Let's again look at the pig's house. If you look up the synonym for house, within the word - house, you find home. When you look at home within the same resource, you find words like: location, situation, mansion, and palace. But if you continue, see house is shelter, retreat, refuge, haven, and then as you keep going it says, eleemosynary institution. What? As you keep going past this word, you see the word "mental institution." A mental institution is a house.

Wait a minute, "did we just say mental institution?" Mental deals with your mind. Institution deals with your governing or primary behaviors. You, your habitat, your natural habitat and environment, your house and inner self are all governed by the same thing. The equalization or balance of the thoughts you hold in your mind and its relationship to your spirit or inner self.

Let's take mind and use it to replace the house the little pig built. The pig built a house or mindset of straw, and the wolf blew it down.

When you look up wolf, we see that the wolf is part of the dog family. Dog is a synonym of wolf. When someone is doggish, it means they are in some way or form, a villain or a scandal. Have you ever heard the term, "he's a dog" or "he's a villain" meaning that he's no good or a cheat. So let's look at wolf as "cheat", or something "no good". When you are dealing with ideas, thoughts and self-awareness, these are all the things that make or break you, if you have a straw mindset it isn't very sturdy. The wolf, the no good and negative thoughts can just huff and puff, until it blows down or away good thoughts, positive ideas – it completely expels it. These are storms, challenges and situations in life, which take us off our mark.

These thoughts apply a blow to it, a slap, a punch, or a hit to your straw foundation and your mental institution. The straw foundation of your mind gets knocked down by doubt, lack of confidence, and other thoughts that enter into your head.

Now there was a second pig. The second pig uses sticks, and sticks still aren't strong enough to stand up against the blows of the wolf. Again these are blows to your mental institution at your foundation. Some of the synonyms for stick are confusion, puzzle, bewilder, perplex, baffle and stump. Sticks mean words and thoughts that confuse, puzzle and bewilder you. These thoughts are perplexing. They leave you baffled and stump your creativity and ideas. The stick foundation does not work.

It's only when you get to the third pig, who applies the concrete or brick mindset – the foundation that I know who I am, I know what I'm going to do, and I'm not going to let anything cheat me out of greatness. I won't let self-doubt, second thoughts or procrastination knock down the solid fortress of my mind, which I've set in stone.

Have you ever tried to have an argument with a person whose mind is set in stone? It is unmovable.

It is unbendable. They won't budge. You must have a stone-like, success mindset, which is set on good for you and the things you want to accomplish.

You cannot let the wolf of procrastination eat your ideas or your beliefs. You cannot let the wolf of procrastination eat your dreams, your visions, or the goals you want to accomplish. You must create a solid foundation in your mind in which you can build upon.

Remember, when the pig built the house of stone. The wolf huffed and puffed, but the house was so strong that the wolf gave up and went away. The same will happen for you. Pretty soon, procrastination won't even come your way. Self-doubt will not pay you a visit. You will get an idea or a thought about a solution to a problem and act on it. Nothing will tempt you. This is because your mind is a fortress for your good. You will be able to do whatever you desire. You will become a doer. You must field the dreams of your mind. You must start. Just take a leap of faith.

When you see the variables E and the equal sign, this means that E is equivalent to something. So the formula of E= means whatever it is on the other side of = is what you become. Your E (energy) or that inner God constantly moves as ideas and thought. Thoughts are things and active things moving constantly. For every action or thought, there is a reaction whether you are conscious of it or not, it never stops. This is the real knowledge behind the Law of Cause and Effect. So what is it that makes you E? How do we connect to this equality of such a powerful concept? Well, let's find out.

CHAPTER 7
M=Mass

CHAPTER 7 – M=MASS

Mass is the body's resistance to being accelerated by a force.

What does water, a human, a star/the sun, a planet, a solar system, and universe all have in common? Give up? **Hydrogen**. They all are made of hydrogen.

They all need each other, which is what makes them one. But also, they are mass. Mass is in almost everything, and the weight of mass varies.

You see, it is easier to pick up a baby human than it is to pick up a baby elephant. It's easier to fall in love than it is to fall out of love – well, for most. A bad idea whose mass grows can literally make you feel heavy, where a good idea enlightens you and is light on you.

Let's look at another movie. Remember the movie Inception. The character of Dominic only had to plant a little seed of doubt in order for them to wake and continue with the thought that was implanted. A little seed of anything negative can grow, and grow, and grow until it ends in tragedy. It can become so strong that you can't even bear it anymore and find yourself susceptible to the implanted thought.

Let's look at stress. Stress can literally ruin a day. In fact, stress can ruin a life. Some have even claimed the weight of stress had given them physical problems, illnesses, and caused weight gain. They feel they're literally carrying this weight or stress on their shoulders. In addition, stress has caused internal problems to where some say their heart hurts. Imagine that. A thought could affect your physical health. Worrying over bills, money or a job could cause you to slowly feel as if someone is stacking brick by brick on top of their shoulders.

On the opposite side of that, the idea of joy, love, laughter and completing a goal can become so strong that it becomes contagious. It is impossible to be upset around a person who carries around that kind of energy. It is magnetizing. This person is always smiling, and it seems as if everything is continually going right for this person. They carry a vibe so strong that it is almost impossible for you to ever be upset with them.

The idea of love is another such thought. Love can be so strong that it almost controls you. Some people lose themselves in others. Some people grow into better people. Some people do crazy things. While others allow love to lead them into great things.

One of the definitions of mass is body. Our body is mass. Therefore, we must understand that our bodies as mass are affected by energy (E). Energy enters into our bodies through inner thoughts and outer thoughts. Outer thoughts are sent through words.

Our inner thoughts can be good or bad. It is based on what we allow to access our mind. If we allow the old friends of procrastination and fear to enter, we get the results from them. Remember I said friend procrastination. See procrastination doesn't seem harmful. It is even comfortable in some eyes. They procrastinate so much and put off so much that nothing ever gets done. Then, they get comfortable never getting things done.

Fear is another one of those *fake friends*. It can be so extreme that it holds you in place forever. Have you heard people joke and say, "I was so afraid, I couldn't move? I was shocked with fear." There are some people who even faint from fear. Fear is strong and many times you might not even know it's there until it suddenly arises inside of you. In reality FEAR is just a false thought we allow in our minds and it is not real. Yet, by giving it power, Energy or thought, it becomes so real, even damaging.

Now the study of mass, like energy, can go on forever, but for the theory of relativity's sake, we will use mass and relativity. Relativistic mass is a total quantity of energy in a body or a system.

It is the total quantity of energy in a body or a system? Hmm, that's interesting. Okay, let's move on. Is the energy functioning in a body or a system? This relativistic mass of a body or system of bodies includes a contribution from kinetic energy of the body, and is largely based on how fast the body moves. The different between relevant mass or relevant body such as a relevant person, depends on the person's frame of reference. The difference is based on a frame of reference.

Let's look at a frame of reference. Wikipedia says in physics, AFR – a frame of reference – is a coordinate system or set of axis within, which measures the position and other properties in it. Stop right there. So the M in mass says to be relevant you must first coordinate a system or set of axis. Alright, let's go back to the synonym finder, and this time, we're going to look up **coordinate**. Coordinate means a correspondent, complementary, equivalent, synonymous, and tantamount. You continue to go down and you see counterpart, equivalent, match, and twin. And when you get to number 4, you see that coordinate means arrange, range, order, dispose, place, or group, to sort out, to assort, to systematize.

We're going to take **arrange.** Looking at a coordinate system, we're going to arrange a system. When looking up system, it says an order, organization, arrangement, and disposition. It also says process, procedure, attack, approach, and other words like a plan of action or a scheme of design. So, we come to two conclusions, we must arrange a plan or design, and set the axis within.

You must have the axis points. Points are tips, projections, and points of time in your life. Points are also point to significance, spirit, aim, objective, goals, and motivation, just to name a few. Stop right there. To become relevant, you must have AFR and to having AFR means you must have a coordinate system or set access points within. The conclusion is you must coordinate or arrange your life. You must create a plan of action with access points meaning plans and goals with both short-term and long-term goals.

Having such a plan of action with goals, helps you become relevant to yourself. It gives you a plan of action for which to do anything you desire. It also helps bring your ideas into action. Now hold it right there. Whoever thought that mass and relativity would be directly connected to goals, aims and action plans? We have all heard of creating goals and plans, but never knew they were mandatory for life and success. They are necessary to tapping into our inner power and creating greatness. Without them, we simply exist. We go about life aimlessly wondering why things keep happening to us. It is because we have no life plan. This really brings new life to "If you fail to plan, you plan to fail." This is right there in $E=mc^2$.

Immediately while researching all of this I thought about what I learned in school. I was never told anything about $E=mc^2$ meaning any of this. I never really thought about E=MC2 at all.

In looking at mass, as the body, we find that we are not only made of energy, but it affects us in so many ways. It makes us feel heavy and it makes us feels light. It is used as a source of success and the lack of energy leads to the lack of success.

When mass (the body) allows itself to align with Energy (E) in a positive way a difference is made, which taps into the spirit.

You can gain 300 pounds, and you can lose those 300 pounds with a simple thought pattern that you implant. You are on the way to becoming the bomb. The new awesome you is waiting to make your acquaintance. You are on the verge of an explosion. But it is you that must cause the explosion. If you are asking, "how do I get to my explosion? Well, remember we said you become more relative with movement. Then that's exactly what needs to happen. **YOU MOST MOVE**. You are currently a sleeping bomb, and this is how you wake up.

You MUST Move and move with the SPEED of LIGHT.

CHAPTER 8
C is for Light

CHAPTER 8 – C IS FOR LIGHT

Earlier, I asked you to remember: *if you build it, they will come for it.* Now notice, the statement says, "if you build it - not when". Once you have made your plan of action, what's next? You may have done this already, but, is it just sitting there gathering dust. You must apply movement and action with the speed of light to accomplish this desired result.

C is light. Light in itself is a separate book, but consider this. We have always been shown the mental, thoughts, or ideas as light. I sat here thinking about the days of cartoons, when one of the characters had an idea, what happened? A light bulb would come above their head. Do you think this was done for no reason? Why a light bulb? Why not a penguin, or a bucket? Well when you go back to the Synonym Finder and you look up light, you see illumination, radiation, shining, beaming, glow, glowing. Then you move on and you see enlightenment, awareness, edification, insight, and understanding.

When we were children, we would often see cartoon characters with the light bulb above their heads. It meant they have received some insight, ideas or an understanding on how to do something. I want you to also take this into consideration, when they did get the ideas, it was from them being silent and going within themselves. By just sitting there and thinking for a moment. It was by being still and knowing they had the answers within.

A light bulb coming above the head means to figure out a situation by an idea coming to light in the mind. They gathered inner sight.

Luckily for us, we happen to live in what is called the information era. We have the internet. We have libraries. We have smartphones. We have all kinds of ways to get information immediately. You can go on YouTube and teach yourself how to do anything these days.

As you make your plans, set the access points, and start moving towards your goal. Trust yourself. You have internal help. Start teaching yourself. Just start the action. The ideas will come and you will have everything you need.

Make sure you introduce procrastination to the front door, because he may have never seen the front of your mind. Once procrastination is at the front door, kick him out and lock the door behind him. Never let him back in. Then turn immediately around and go to work. Know that with a locked door and closed the windows, nothing can stop you. There will be no negativity that can stand against you. Only allow the illuminated thoughts and ideas to enter your mind.

If you knew that you could do anything, and it would not fail what would you do? This is what you **are** able to do when you use your inner power. You create and cause its existence.

Light means to ignite. So going back to the idea of the power of a bomb, when you are in a situation, you can create the change you want by understanding you have the power. You have picked up this book. The information has now dropped in your lap and hit you right in the middle of your forehead. The more you read, the more light enters your mind. Your thoughts are speeding up.

TNT is TNT. It may look harmful, but unless a fuse is lit, it is just completely stagnate. It takes some action. It needs to be lit. It has to have light. You too must have a light to get going. Step out of on faith. Just do it.   An idea like most dinners are both best served hot. When you get an idea, you must do it right away.

You may not have all the confidence at first. Yet, the power is still there waiting for you to do something with it.   It is your choice whether you light the fuse or not. However, if you do decide to take that lead of faith, there is something I want to share with you that may literally change your life forever.

CHAPTER 9
Squared

CHAPTER 9 – SQUARED

Becoming Squared Up...

When you light up and with practice you will light up quickly, you will realize that miracles will start to happen. Some people call this, "A series of rapid coincidences". The faster the speed or rather the faster the need, the faster your goals will be accomplished. You need to understand you are dealing with pure power, pure knowledge. You are squaring yourself with your inner-G, with the inner God. You are squaring yourself with the divine source.

To be square means a quadrant or be a part of something, pacify, make peace, to come to terms, to patch up, to mend, and to clear. The definition goes on to say, to straighten and to level, and to even. When you square yourself, you're evening yourself. You are making yourself even. You are balancing yourself. You are coming to terms with yourself and with your inner-G.

Many people face what some would call impossible odds. One lady through a series of random events all in the course of about a month faced these types of impossible odds. The house she was renting was foreclosed, leaving her to have to move in a month. She had car payments due, meetings for business opportunities, where she needed to travel across the country. Her sister was getting married and she was in the wedding. This wedding was not close to her home or the business meeting. She had no idea how she would get to either of the two places, or where she would live in the next month. She had children to support, a stressed out husband, and she had absolutely no money for a down payment on a new place to live.

She began to ask questions, many questions. All of these questions were asked of herself. She asked herself what to do to make all of this work. She told herself she would be open to all answers. She inadvertently taught herself to be open and conscious to any assistance. More importantly, she left her little meditative prayer, confident things would work out. She knew of a surety help would come – and it did. Her help came in her husband's business picking up. It came in her picking up little jobs locally, when she got an idea and was referred by friends. These referrals were so prosperous it turned into a home business. A friend with airline points offered to take care of her trip and vacation, while she did business. Her small account easily paid for a ticket and all expenses for the wedding. Was this a coincidence or miracle? It solely depends on what you believe. This lady was actively working with the formula of $E=mc^2$. She used the formula masterfully and never looked back.

Some would say, "Oh this is a coincidence." I think not. This lady was simply conscious. She was conscious of the power within herself. She applied action to every idea and got her husband to do the same.

Everything in life is squared. Clouds bring forth rain. The rain comes down. It evaporates and becomes clouds again. Even the animals are squared, and they know their connection to spirit.

Now let me shape the foundation of this new world of thought. What I'm about to tell you is so important for you to know, and if you don't believe anything else that has been said in this book, I need you to understand this.

Everything is squared. This includes people and every idea. Ideas are both squared and in motion. Ideas are squared because they pacify, balance, and fulfill a need. Remember ideas are energy. They are in motion. Because ideas are in motion, how can an idea be yours unless you claim it? An idea is just that – an idea. It is the Energy (E). Ideas need a host. The host is Mass. The Mass is you. An idea is a type of energy which doesn't know or care, what you did or what you're doing now. An idea's goal is to manifest – that's it. When it does, guess what? The idea is complete. The idea goes and tells other ideas that we are a willing host. Just like when you see a great movie or eat at a great restaurant, you go and you tell a friend and you recommend it. You become a source for ideas. This is because you are willing to take **ACTION.**

When an idea comes to a person and the person utilizes it, the idea becomes a beacon to other ideas saying, "hey guys, I have a host. He works for me; maybe he'll work for you". Then more ideas come to you to be manifested. Hence the saying, "the rich get richer and the poor get poorer." See you can be rich in thoughts and ideas. Remember I said, "You are a live wire, for positive or negative". Whatever you're focused on, you become a vessel for it.

Do you disagree? Well, have you ever had an idea about something? Have you ever thought about something you should do? Have you thought of something that would be beneficial or helpful, then a year later you see it on a TV infomercial. Maybe, you see it a few years later and you think to yourself, "I was just thinking about that a year or two ago, but I didn't do anything about it."

Or you think, "I'm going to change my life for the better". You start focusing on your health and a goal to lose weight. You do it a little while then you stop. Months later you look up and someone you know has dropped 40 or 50 pounds and they look good.

See the idea came to you, but you didn't square it. Square means you put all faith, hope and action into what you do. See if you don't take massive action on ideas squared in your mind, you will start something but not finish. Energy (E) are ideas that need a host, speed and squaring in the mind. They are built of strong brick or concrete like foundations.

We have on average about 60,000 thoughts per day. Thousands of them are creative thoughts and ideas. What would you do with a thousand creative ideas that would potentially be life changing? What would you do? How would your life change with just three creative life changing ideas?

Many people's lives have changed with one creative idea. Remember, an idea is not entitled to you; it is just looking for a host.

Remember, we all have the God spirit. We all have the opportunity to become squared. We are all spirit. So if your mind doesn't accept the idea, know someone is going to grab your idea and, they will be a host for it.

The idea first came to you, but you didn't do anything about it. You didn't help it to manifest. It came to you first and found out you were too busy. So, it had to find someone who would do the work.

If you build it (the active, strong and faithful mind), they (the ideas) will come. The key is you must build it. If the Wright brothers don't build the planes, do you not think someone would've thought to fly? Yes. The idea would have gone to someone else. If you don't gather up the courage to do what's needed, someone else will. It is crazy to think the whole world is motion, but ideas stop with you. Someone is going to have to fill the void of none action.

Think of life as a highway. You're driving on this freeway of life. While you're riding on this freeway, maybe you just slow down a little bit. Do you not think that ahead of you people are changing lanes, or people behind you are changing lanes? If you slow down, people will go around you. People cut in front of you. People take up the space. That's how life is. That's how energy is also. Being a live wire, if you're not a host for the ideas, the ideas go and find a host.

Aren't you tired of being that person – the one with all the great ideas, but with no action behind it? They're your ideas, so why can't you manifest them? What is wrong with you? How are you not capable of doing it?

You are. You are very capable, and up until this point you have been watching others live your dreams – yes you. You have been watching others live your dreams, or walk with a body like the one you want, live the life you have once seen for yourself.

Remember, we are all energy – all of us. So, the next person is just as deserving as you. Since we are squared, we also possess another power. Deep down you probably all know and have been saying all your life, but you did not know what it was. You thought it was coincidence.

On your journey to recognizing your new powers and becoming one with them, you need to have someone to work with you. Having someone in your corner as an accountability partner and keeping you accountable can generate speed of light, squared. This is what causes the explosion. Squared is the end of the formula.

Everything you desire and all you wish for is all around you. You just have to look for the signs. When generating this explosive idea, you generate the speed by putting your action in motion, and the people you need, will just magnetize towards you. See we are all synced. The people you need will literally just appear out of nowhere. They will be there willing and able to supply you with what you need.

You must coordinate or arrange a system, arrange a course or align a plan of action. Make sure you create your access points, which means make goals. You must grab the ideas that pop up in your mind, create a plan of action with goals and go to work manifesting. You may become relevant in whatever area you like. Let the ideas flow.

One more thing, for those of you who thought was $E=MC^2$ was only used to make a hydrogen bomb. Well you are half right. You are just not looking deeply enough. It's you. You – yes you – are literally the bomb. You are a walking, talking, explosion of power. You are awesome.

So now you're probably thinking, "Well, where the heck is my explosion?" In many cases, the fuse is just not lit. While it is true you are a bomb. You are a sleeping bomb, and this is how you wake up.

CHAPTER 10

Stop, Drop, and Roll

CHAPTER 10 - STOP, DROP, and ROLL

You are on fire! You are on fire. Stop, Drop, and Roll!

Once you make your new moves, everyone sees it. Everyone notices the changes. The difference in your center being is radiating. All of your energy is magnetizing. It's all connected. Now it's time for you to know this. The obstacles are coming. They have to, because you cracked the code.

You have to prove to yourself, you really want it. Now don't get confused. It's you doing it. It's the new recognized inner you making sure of what you want and making sure you want it bad enough.

Remember, your faith and belief in your new found information will be tested. Procrastination sees you out there with an idea. Since you haven't called or haven't returned any of his messages. It watches you carefully. You have blocked all of his emails. You have moved on. Not only have you moved on, but you've moved on at light speed. You've got all your goals set. You've got all your points crossed, and you're just moving up towards your dreams.

Consider this, if you are on a road to success let's say it begins in San Francisco, and it finishes in New York. Do you expect to drive straight across with no problems, curves or detours? Absolutely there will be challenges. There are many different roads, many different terrains. You might have weather issues. There might be stops. There may be bridges to cross. Hopefully, you have a great car. If not, you might have engine problems. You might need some tires. You might have to drive off-road a little bit. You could get lost. The people in the car that's been with you since the beginning might start to annoy you. All kinds of shenanigans could occur.

If you have ever played the game, The Oregon Trail. You are aware that you will run into roadblocks. It is not easy, but nothing great ever is. Know when you're on the trip from San Francisco to New York some thoughts may have to get dropped off and go back to San Francisco, because they get homesick.

They may say, "You know what, I like the way things were. When we were led by procrastination, we didn't have to hurry like this", they could give up. But, make sure you don't give up. They could mentally fall back asleep and forget the formula. However, do not allow yourself to do this. You might be on the open road, where thieves and looters try to steal dreams. But, you must protect them, even if that means letting go of old thoughts and old ways.

Remember in the beginning I told you, you must have the brick mindset. You might encounter periods where you're closest friends or family might challenge you. You must remain strong and consistent. There's power in a secret. Often, that power comes from not sharing your ideas with others until they have manifested.

Look at every success story you've ever heard or read about. Everyone loves a good success story. Look at the movies, "The Pursuit of Happiness", with Will Smith, who was sleeping in the bathroom with his son. He lived hotel to hotel just trying to find a way to endure. There is the word: endure.

You must *endure* on your journey. You must endure to the end. You must endure until your idea comes into manifestation. You're going to have times when you don't want to go to the gym, but you must continue and you must endure. Remember, equation and everything shared. Think of the story the Tortoise and the Hare. The Hare took off and he was gone. Some people will start off fast. Some people will just build up so much momentum. The hare had speed. The tortoise had the power to endure. It may sound like a children's tale, but it is really what goes on every single day. It goes on all around you.

We must have the momentum and the endurance. People get ideas, they get super excited about it and when they put energy into an idea, it will take off.

The secret to ignite your fuse is create – Enthusiasm. Enthusiasm is the interior fire created by excitement, zeal and happiness. It will build speed. Ideas love enthusiasm. They will throw a party for enthusiasm, all day. It will start to just grow and grow, but you must keep it up. Know your ideas are already being manifested and be excited about it. Be excited about the little coincidences you get. Be excited about the little wins. Be excited about the big wins.

You can't take the obstacles personally, it is you generating them. One thing I learned is everyone comes into the light, or the info they need to progress at their own time.

You must stop, drop, and roll. You must stop; assess the situation, obstacle or problem. Drop it below you and worry no more. You're in control of the problems. So they're not over you. They can't be. Once you stop, drop then next you roll. You're on fire with your ideas. Stop, Drop, and Roll.

Roll means exactly what it sounds like. Roll over the speed-bumps. Roll through issues, because really, they are faith checks. It's just your energy saying, "do you really want this as bad as you say you do?"

I'm not saying expect crazy things, I'm just saying don't rule them out. Don't let them crush your momentum or your energy. Don't resort to being distraught or saying you cannot do something. Let your enthusiasm keep you on fire. The reason why the idea came to you is because you could do it. You are able. You are able and you are resurrected mentally, so things are going to come. Don't be distraught or surprised by challenges – stop, drop, and roll. Assess the situation, drop it below you, and roll over it, if needed. You're going to have an excellent story to tell by the end of it.

Eventually, these faith checks will come less and less, because you won't need them. Simply put say, "Okay, I believe you." Just like that, they will come to a minimum, until eventually it become dust on the shoulder. Now, here comes the *bang*.

Chapter 11

The Adam Bond
The Theory of Being Relative

CHAPTER 11 - THE ATOM BOMB/THE THEORY OF BEING RELATIVE

E=MC2 is known as the *theory of relativity*.

In practical terms, what is $E=mc^2$ relative to? Relativity is the ability to relate. It is being Relative to yourself and the world to the Inner G inside of you. You are literally adjusting yourself to a God-like frequency.

Energy equals an idea, information, or light on that idea. Squaring refers to the squaring of your mind to prepare it for use to yourself and others. It is the ability to work an idea with the speed of light; therefore, creating an explosion of energy within and all around you.

This power can be used for any idea. Rather it is for losing weight, curing yourself, acquiring something you want, fulfilling a destiny, finding the right person or building a business, you are your own answer. There is no one more powerful than you. You are the one who has enough energy inside to power a whole city. You are the Atom Bomb. You hold all this power. You are the one who is bonded or connect to the All-Powerful Source. Theologians call it God. Scientists call it Energy. I tell you now that it is God, Energy, Spirit and Power.

This $E=mc^2$ is very relative. It relates to you in every way. It is all things and in all things. It is the Law of Cause and Effect. It is the cause and it effects. It is the Law of Attraction. It is the source of the way things are attracted to us. It is the source and reason for all thought. It is the Law of Gravity. It is the reason gravity exists. It's all things in this world and beyond.

This power is always in motion. It is never still. You too cannot stand still. Even if your body is still, your thoughts are in motion. Since your thoughts are in motion, you're always attracting. You are attracting positive or negative energy. It depends on what you are putting out. You have just as much or more power than the physical Atom bomb. You will explode positive power, if you give off positive thoughts. You will explode negative power, if you give out negative thoughts. You are the Power.

Continue to ask yourself questions and listen for the answer. Continue giving yourself marriage counseling. Yes, you are married to yourself and your mental philosophies. Sit down and write out the terms to bettering your relationship with yourself.

IF IT ISNT WRITTEN,
IT DOES NOT EXIST.

Do daily self-checkups. Ask the questions of yourself.

1. **Am I sleeping with the enemy?**
2. **What do I need?**
3. **What ideas am I working towards?**
4. **Am I being truthful in my work efforts?**

I started studying to get the info for E=MC2 on a whim. It was something that called to me. It spoke to me and through me. It wanted its voice heard. It came as an idea. The more I studied it, the more in engulfed me and the more it changed me.

The equation is something you must live, so I just started to put it into motion. In a matter of days my life changed so much. After 30 days, the change was apparent and contagious. Everyone around me noticed it. They began to ask questions about what I was doing and how I was doing it.

That's when I decided I would go out to help and show others this amazing key to success. I knew it was something practical and easy to utilize. I made the decision to take the leap of faith and just start changing my life. I had made some significant progress and many changes. I was excited and enthusiastic about everything I was doing. This new thought, created a new outlook and new habits.

Driven by the power of $E=mc^2$, I decided to share it with my mentor. As we met, I sat and went through the whole plan. I explained what I was going to do. How I would talk about it. How it had worked for me and many others. I gave my checklist, my goals, etc. She just sat there listening attentively. After I finished my full theory and plan, she sat there staring at me. Suddenly, she started to laugh. I slowly felt embarrassment. I could feel negative self-consciousness creeping into my mind. Immediately, I put the man in the doorway. He is the one that stops all unwanted energy. I thought she was ridiculing my evidence or possibly shunning the idea. She went into her office pulled out her notes dated over a year and a half ago.

All of her notes were on the equation $E=MC2$. She had started it, had done a little work, but she STOPPED. She had done some research and writing, but she STOPPED. She had thought to write this exact book a year and a half before. She freely shared her notes with me and we laughed as we compared notes.

She said she just hadn't found the time to do it. She looked at me smiled and said, "I guess it found a willing host!" She had been a victim of the power of $E=mc^2$. This was a classic example of how the energy will find a source.

This power has been right here in front of us all these years. There is no more advantage for one person than for the other. There is an unlimited supply.

"Behold the People is one and they have all one language and this they begin to do, and now nothing will be restrained to them which they have imagined to do." This means whatever you imagine to do, you can accomplish.

NOTHING WILL BE RESTRAINED FROM YOU

While others may seem to have an advantage at times, it really is only the frequency in which they are vibrating. It's all attraction and you have been doing it unconsciously all this time.

ASK AND YOU SHALL RECEIVE

However you have come by this information now, please know that it is not by coincidence. Nothing is. You sent out a beacon, which in turn warranted a response and brought you here.

PROCRASTINATION KILLS CREATION

You are now on the clock! It is time to stop letting opportunities fade from you and start visualizing and materializing. Remember an idea is not married to you until you put in the work.

We must understand the power of Energy (E). To sum it all up Energy is the sum total of all we think and do. Energy controls it all. The E in the formula holds so much power that its symbol is used very cautiously. The letter E represents a force that is comprehendible and yet incomprehensible simultaneously.

POWER OF AN ATOM

Atoms are pure energy. Atoms are composed of particles called protons, electrons and neutrons. Protons carry a positive electrical charge, electrons carry a negative electrical charge, and neutrons carry a neutral charge. These particles represent the positive, negative and neutral thoughts. In the physical world these thoughts interact with each other to produce the things focused on.

Scientists used atoms and constructed a destructive device that obliterated miles of terrain and its inhabitants. But remember there is always an equal to all things. There is another side to this destructive power. It is an equal power of good. When you follow the steps of $E=mc^2$, you hold both. You have the power to construct an incredible new life for yourself, or you have the choice to use your power to become a destructive force. You can make your life plan and create the goals to the life you desire, or you can fail to plan and continue to let life happen to you.

You control the outcome. You dictate the relationship. You have the power. You are the Power.

E>mc²

Energy represents both the seen and the unseen. Its power is in the known and unknown. It is the all-powerful, unlimited creative force in the universe and beyond. Therefore, it can actually be said that Energy (E) is actually greater than mass times speed squared. It is in fact, the Inner (G), the Inner God.

You must remember you are connected to your newly discovered God-self. We are all also connected to the source of **ALL POWER**. You can use your great power to create the life and peace of mind you desire.

In this book, you have been introduced to this power. It is up to you to study it and apply the steps to your life. It is up to you to TAKE this power and create an amazing life. It is up to you to apply the steps of

E=mc². It is up to YOU. However, know this for surety that if you do not to do it, someone else will.

References

English Wikipedia Free Encyclopedia. (2013). Retrieved February-March 2013, from Wikipedia Web site: www.wikipedia.org

Hill, N. (1968, 2012). *Master Keys to Riches.* Dover Publications.

Rodale, J. (1978). *Synonym Finder.* New York: Warner Books by permission of Rodale Press, Inc.

Yahweh, Y. (2012). *Super Mind.* www.thirddaystore.com: Third Day Productions.

www.ingramcontent.com/pod-product-compliance
Lightning Source LLC
Chambersburg PA
CBHW071006040426
42443CB00007B/688